A DOG CALLED INSTEAD

Noel Frances Murphy

To all the human people who read poems written by human people

Contents

I was telling a friend a short while ago that some of the poems I've put in this collection date back to the 1980s, which for me isn't that far at all. Until I think about it. However, the date of conception is rarely the date that I've assigned to any of the poems here.

Nor is the poem given the date of the final word or punctuation mark. Some get dated to the time that I recognised them as poems rather than notes made on forms of paper or screen time. Some get the date when I decided that I liked them.

Unlike life, because poems are unlike life, a poem starts out as a skeleton and then fattens up before heading off on its own into the world. Or sometimes the other way around.

I didn't used to think like that. I used to sit down and say, "I'm writing a poem about how steam engines were invented even though steam wasn't". Then I'd set to it using lots of imagery about steam and fire and water and metals and time and inventors.

My god, I'd drown in adjectives and similes, and

why the hell not? No one told me any differently. In fact, no one paid any attention at all to poems, my poems, and why the hell should they, those ghosts?

You should have seen my crepuscular petrichors and my purple bruised sunsets and my achingly awfully ailing alignments of alliterative alignments of stardust saddled solutions (which we are all made of). There were notebooks full of the stuff before I put them all in a fire one night somewhere between Bristol and Bath.

An event I've never regretted, although I wouldn't recommend it.

A lot of my poetry moves about, sometimes geographically, sometimes meaningfully, sometimes formally. Actually, all of it does. I've never produced a fully formed poem not even as a teenager when this compulsion first made itself known; and when, by all that is holy, it should have laid down and died a sad, tearful adolescent death.

Now, however, I'm in my 50s and still producing poems. Why the fuck would I do that? Sometimes for salve and sometimes for salvation. Mostly because I've just never stopped, and it just keeps coming. What can you do about that.

The poems in this selection veer between enormous sadness, and the many attempts I've made to resolve that (or those) into a life force, to silliness or wordplay or just experimentation. I've left the love poems out because they'll need another collection for themselves because that's what romantic love is like I think.

In terms of place well:

Reading (a suitable name for a book of poetry, I'll have to do something with that) was a terrible old place that followed Twyford – where my dad died and I was in my teens – and Winchester.

London, there are no London poems in this collection. London needs a special book of its own because London is where I discovered loneliness, booze and the nightbus – like a lot of people do.

Sydney was happy until my wife and I separated

and our daughter died. All that is a longer story, of course. But you'll get a flavour of my state from the Sydney poems I think.

Wakefield was a strange place: the first time there was drunk. Filthy drunk then fatherhood and work and the diagnosis of our daughter's condition. The second time there was following my time in Australia. Again drunk but this was 20 years later and the drink was ground in and grinding like broken glass in a gutter.

York is where I am now with my second wife. I don't really bother with the booze nowadays. Diabetes and nerve destruction have taken away the thrill. Also, I reckon I've got less than twenty years to go before death comes along and really gets me out of my head. So, why waste the time that's left?

I hope you enjoy these poems that come from the same teenage, prime time, middle and older aged person who isn't the same at all. And you can read these in any order you like.

2023

York

White Crow

In the frost this morning
I saw a white crow
On a post
Arguing with a ghost of a robin.
"There is nothing more delicious than carrion"
Said Crow.
"There is nothing better than fighting"
Said Ghost.
Having caught Crow's black eye.
Having caught Ghost's ire.
I walked on across the field
Embarrassed by my own eavesdropping.

2022

York

Crisp Snow

Beer breaths
Under a bridge
With friends
Vinegar skin
Outside
The chip shop
We were full
Loud music
Inside
The new Club
We all dance
New shoes
Inside
Hospital
We relax.

1987

Reading

Lines in a textile mill

A man in a white suit
cobbles outside my chapel flat
smoking up the room
as whisky children make
sleep improbable.

The factory lights went out
and the rain has stopped too.
The women came out on strike
which, like the men,
didn't help at all.

Instead the money built
a chapel, my flat where I smoked
sunk in alcoholic bad television
with the echoes of singing
hymns to mercy.

2006

Wakefield

A Dog Called Instead

I was going to enter the TS Eliot Poetry Prize

A dog called instead

A god called Achilles Christ Jesus McGrew

Ate my entry form

The form was chewed by Achilles Christ Jesus McGrew

A fireworks store in Mayfair

So

blue

red orange

green

sparkles and explosive awe

So loud and raw like Saint Peter screaming before Christ
the rock

Store.

No entry form for my damned entry

because of Ulysses Jesus Christ McGraw

Denied a thread from a veil, and gumboots in my Edenic
garden

No, not with a banger

But by a whippet

Amen be with you

        (and also with you dog also with you)

2007

Wakefield

Lucky Boy

Lucky boy rescued
Gave me this picture
At the start of a long Spring evening.
Lovely rescued boy
Corners on a sixpence
Barking, bouncing ball
Lovely boy jumps up
Runs and rescues
Everything he can around him.

2016

York

Gravity is a pitiless hard worker

Up Version

Even high mountains are conquered
By gravity
Because gravity is a pitiless hard worker
Stopping stepping sidestepping boots
To no end.
This poem is spoken in a voice like a straight canal
Up and down – up and down
Locked
That poem was destroyed by high eagles
Up and down up and down
eerie
Up and down up and down like mountains
Up and down up and down like voices
Up and down like eagles
Cold as isolation
Hot as an oven chip
On and on like train tracks, rocket ships, clown trousers,
love, arrows and forgetting.
Because Gravity is a pitiless hard worker.

Gravity is a pitiless hard worker

Down version

The high mountains are conquered
By gravity
Because gravity is a hard worker.
Up and down
like clown trousers
love arrows and forgetting.

2016

York

Girls Skipping at Easter

When I see the black and white,
The grey photograph
of young girls skipping
in Alciston, East Sussex in 1952
with sign for Tamplin's Brewery
hanging behind them
All in mid air
they are wearing
winter coats
soon to be cast off for joy
a flat capped old man
holds one end
of the rope near the pub smiling
at the other side of the frame
the rope disappears into space
I think of young girls in ghettos
Like Watts or Warsaw
it's the nature of photographs.
It's the nature of skipping.
It's nature of play,
for fun, in the spring
that should only end
in summer and in love.

2023

York

The boats

So, the boat
'The Holy Roller'
or
'The Devil's Dingy'
or
'Salvation'
or
'Damnation'
made it, sluggish, into the bay
broken masts and men
in the early sunlight.
There were fists raised against it
by savages from the shore.
Back in South Sudan, in Kabul.
and in Syria,
in, you name the lost place,
hearts beat faster
and breaths are drawn short,
ignorant of the outcome.
Delicious meals were eaten
as the missing souls,
on 'The Rubber Raft' or 'The Heartbreaker',
were discussed and wine was taken.
as waves beat down
on their unmercied souls.

Alan and Galip Kurdi are on the beach
still now
waiting for 'The Heaven Sent' or 'The Floating Hope'
or some way to get to get a lung of air
inside them to feed them
to sit them up and place them safely
into a country of civilised people
not pampered savages with flags for souls.

2022

York

The snowflakes

Every snowflake is uni…
Stop now before you spout one this out.
Remember that everything in nature is unique.
That snowflake revelation is
nothing to shake a beech leaf at,
nothing to make a claggy lamb's tail rise.
That fly on the elephant's
eyeball whipped by an eyelash
exiting without dignity on the afternoon wind,
also unique.

2023

York

The fall

The leaves are coming back
But you're not here again.
Of course
I understand
but I find it hard to walk
where I walked
when I pushed you along
in your chair.

But at least the leaves are here again.
For now the shade they make
will bless my skin.

Until the fall comes
Across my solitary walk
when those leaves come down
To cover and quiet me again.

2022

York

Redactio ab adsurbum

Loves can be summed up
in a few words
on blocks of colour
to be shared for Likes.
Explain your real
and genuine pain
your arrhythmic heartache
to nodding echoes
at lost likes
or loves
It's cute
and completely reasonable
to attract the attention of strangers
like a hitchhiker begging a lift to
your next location.

2023

York

Star gazey pi

All the stars are rowdy tonight
exploding and simultaneously sucking
everything around them.
In time as real as we can imagine.
Such violent tenderness.
Such monstrous need.

Every planet trusts the gravity
of everything around it.
Every moon moves gently
mooning over its lover.
Having bruised it once
it yearns to surrender.

2004

Sydney

Bordering on

The border is
A leaf falling down
On a fence
Balancing and
Being pulled by each side
Being blown from side to side
Over and over again
Until next year
And they pull again.
And they blow again.
And the leaf it falls again
Year after year.
Onto the border.
Helpless but inevitable
Until they cut down the tree
To make another fence.

2005 Sydney
2022 York

The Swing of things

The swing of things
around here
today
resulted in a gap
like love on holiday.
Remarking to you
around there that day
that you should smile
was stupid and remiss.
Today
the swing of things
around here
is wearying
like nostalgia for sun in rain.
Around here today
the swing of things
is hanging off its frame
a door in fragments.
The swing of things
Around here
Today
Is not like usual
Around here
the swing of things
today

is a dull, warped plastic bell
A stepless dance
watched by a mob
wearing contempt not contemplation
like part-time animals.

2004

Sydney

A shock to the system

Let us
face it
The shock of the new
is not what we want
right now.
(some times
we do
just not
right now)

What we want
right now
is totally
untaught
humming.
(getting away
from the shock
of our own needs now)

Somethings we can
want but not
for want of
confusion.

What is needed right now

this minute
this moment in time
this hour of the year
this iota of life
this now
not before
not then
is simple, straightforward peace.
hand holding, cake baking, anti-freedom.
What we need right at this exact second
is not another question but more contemplation
of afternoon sunlight
and a gentle background hum.

(before I said the eulogy / I wrote it / shock after shock /
of what it all meant / as each word hit the paper / like a
teardrop / on an anvil / most silent of stages / full of guilt
rage / at the unfairness / of loss shock / after shock upon
shock / like the ambulance siren)

2004
Sydney

Wearing the surplus

1,000 euros of red wine dregs in the curve of a glass
heading to the bottom of a sink
at the bottom of an evening
15 hours long.
It could make you stop and think.

It could be used for the final toast
to the health of the self.

So, wealth is about surplus.
and not what you keep.
It's about throw away lines
slipping away with no second glance.

10,000 dollar bottles of red,
are dug up from Napoleonic floors,
over which 50,000,000 euro malls are raised.
Selling five dollar bottles of wine,
to party people along with their milk and their bread.

Six dollar t-shirts.
One euro mugs.
Ten Thousand Dollar alcohol?
(even the thought is downright lurid)

How?
Do you drink it?
Do you share it with friends?
Do you guzzle it all for yourself?

Someone is rich enough to slob out on the couch,
balls dressed in silk cotton,
crackling sea-salt and basil fried oysters down their y-
fronts
watching bad television,
guzzling 10,000 pound wine from the neck all alone.

2004

Sydney

At 00:17

I will go to sleep
With nothing to say to you or me
And hope tomorrow to be free
Or that the dark will stop that day
As I have nothing more to say
As I have nothing more to say
I will close my eyes today
And hope tomorrow to be free
Or that the dark will have its way
And I will go to sleep
I will go to sleep
With nothing to say to you or me
And the dark will do as it may
As I have nothing more to say
The dark won't ever go away
and light has nothing more to say.

2005

Sydney

At 05:47

Fish to water, the drive to the boat
The bad bait in the car
Before a breakfast of servo sarnies
Lights on huge around us.
Until the harbour split
The engine kicks in
Snapper water, not yet
Kingfish water, not yet
Dolphin, flying fish, not yet.
Our boat lights out
Sun up eyes down
Fluidity, happily with me.
The boat kicks on around us
Our early, fragile spines kicked
Our mouths shut for breakfast.
Then out of the heads to the hold on!
Hold on! Hold on!
That sea, those fish flying below!
That sunlight!
The bad bait
Jettisoned.
We fish for more
We fish.

2002

Sydney

A 08:13

Just a small whisper
like a stranger on the underground
there and not here.
Sitting across from you,
reading or just staring avoidance.
Not a life you recognise
because of everything else
that's going on inside you.
But there for a long city moment
Between stops.

(There, just a whisper
There it is and goes
off and away on nothing more substantial
than the air that you breathe)

There we once were, whispers
Hidden inside conversations
Fragments of cotton fabrications
in deafening wrecks of hallways.
Neither recalled nor forgotten
Just echoes whose origins
Are long delayed.

(There is simply not enough time

to crane a neck closer
to a dear mouth
to concentrate.
Because the days are not alive
Because of everything else)

Listen, a whisper
Maybe two or more
in the clanking inconsideration
of disassembled carriages
just above on the hard oily ground.
There we are or were, fleetingly
Briefly and contentedly
Forever quietly making ourselves heard
To each other for all time at all.

1981

Reading

Zuzu's funeral I

Beyond the peace that flowed from her living sleep
That stopped suddenly
In her bedroom near dawn
Was a hall with a curtain and an oven
For her body
To lift away
As smoke
Into Sydney's contrasting light.

On the perfectly green lawn
Of the modern crematorium
Ice cold filled with fire
In the July winter sun

We were so deeply moved
By your scared kind wishes,
Evaporating in front of us
As we tried to survive the future

As she lay there, ready
I brushed her hair
As I often did before

Although her skull
had been opened

and emptied
and closed
I listened to other people
Behind me talking about her life
because they didn't know.

(Her laughter that was real once
had drifted away
and gone
Imagine that
If you can)

She left pursued by white balloons
Brought along to the scene
By someone I didn't know
Who was doing their very best.

After abnormal handshakes
and crushing embraces
we went down to the pub.
and I started drinking
For decades.

2004 Sydney
2006 Wakefield
2023 York

Zuzu's funeral II

We were so deeply moved
By your scared sacred wishes,
Evaporating in front of us kindly.
As we were trying to survive
the future.
As she lay there, ready
I brushed her hair
As I often did before
Even though her skull
was emptied
opened and re-closed
I listened to other people
Behind me talk about her life.
crying and laughing.

2004 Sydney
2006 Wakefield
2023 York

A nice cuppa tea

(For mum during dementia)
I will make you a cup of tea
The shade you like
The warmth you find comforting
The sweetness you find acceptable
And you'll savour it
And recall all the other cups
In your long, eventful life
And you will be you safe this afternoon
As you drift
As it rains outside
As I say I love you
As I put the cup in your paper skin hand.
Reaching outside of all recognition
As I cease to exist for you
But you're still there
Drinking the tea
That someone kind brought you once.

2013

Southsea

Printed in Great Britain
by Amazon

21358439R00031